One Wintry Night

*A*nd it came to pass
in those days that a decree went out from Caesar Augustus that all the world
should be registered. This census first took place while Quirinius was
governing Syria. So all went to be registered. . . .

And Joseph also went up from Galilee, out of the city of Nazareth,
into Judea, to the city of David, which is called Bethlehem,
because he was of the house and lineage of David, to be registered with Mary,
his betrothed wife, who was with child.

So it was, that while they were there, the days were completed
for her to be delivered. And she brought forth her firstborn Son,
and wrapped Him in swaddling cloths, and laid Him in a manger,
because there was no room for them in the inn.

Now there were in the same country shepherds living out in the fields,
keeping watch over their flock by night. And behold, an angel
of the Lord stood before them, and the glory of the Lord shone around them,
and they were greatly afraid.

Then the angel said to them, "Do not be afraid, for behold I bring you
good tidings of great joy which will be to all people. For there is born to you
this day in the city of David a Savior, who is Christ the Lord."

LUKE 2:1-11

RUTH BELL GRAHAM

One Wintry Night

Illustrated by
RICHARD JESSE WATSON

 Baker Books

A Division of Baker Book House Co
Grand Rapids, Michigan 49516

CAUGHT IN THE STORM CHAPTER 1

The boy hunkered down and yanked his cap further over his ears as the wind rose to a roar across the ridge. Low, dark clouds moving down from the north were bringing darkness early. A snowflake touched his cheek. The boy was mountain tough, but his grandpa had warned him against taking a long hike alone on such a cold day. Still, the boy had the urge.

He loved the mountains—especially the Seven Sisters. They were home to him. He'd lost track of how many times he had hiked them. His grandpa used to climb with him, only grandpa's heart wasn't up to it now.

Another gust of wind caught the boy off balance. Grabbing a tree for support, he lit the old possum lantern against the oncoming darkness. Then, in its flickering yellow glow, he noticed the leaves of the laurel were curled up tight like pencils in the bitter cold.

Again the roar of the wind rose in the bare branches above him. The boy wasn't scared, but for the first time he wondered if he would make it home.

He wasn't only mountain tough, he was mountain smart. He figured he was well past Big Piney now. Then he remembered the cove, the one his great-grandpa had settled. It couldn't be far—on the south side of the ridge between the Big Piney and Stompy Knob. Other folks had bought the property from the mountain family some time ago. His grandpa used to tell stories of how he had helped build the place for them, fetching rocks from the mountain streambeds—even from old still furnaces—for the chimneys and walls.

If the boy could make it down there, they'd let him in.

Inside the log and frame house, the woman heard the dogs bark. Not a friendly bark, but mean and fierce. She turned on the outside lights, peering through the little window by the front door. They were quiet now. But something was going on out there.

The wind sounded like a freight train coming over the ridge, and the snowflakes were blowing sideways instead of falling straight down.

Then she saw them, the two big dogs with a boy walking between, like he'd known them before.

The woman opened the door.

"I'm Zeb Morris," the boy yelled breathlessly as he ran toward the lighted entrance. "My grandpa, he helped build this . . ."

Before he could finish the sentence, the boy stumbled. The woman caught him and helped him inside.

The Boy And The Woman

Next morning the boy woke up and peered drowsily out of the window upon a strange world. Where the sky was usually blue, the clouds were almost black. And where the ridge should have risen dark, it was white and soft. The dark, leafless trees—they, too, were white. And huge snowflakes were falling silently.

Snow always filled the boy with excitement. He jumped from the big bed before noticing how high it was, and nearly cried out in pain. He didn't. But when he looked at the ankle he had twisted last night, he saw it was swollen and blue.

"Doggoneit!" he exclaimed. Now how would he get home? He pulled on all but his left sock and shoe and limped across the hall to what looked to be the kitchen.

"Good morning, Zeb," the woman said.

"Mornin', ma'am," he replied. The smell of frying bacon, fresh coffee and wood smoke made him feel at home.

He stood shyly beside the door, the large gray-and-white-striped cat rubbing against his good leg.

"Lost a shoe?" the woman asked.

"No'm. Comin' down by the old bear's den last evenin' where it's almighty steep, I twisted it. Didn't really notice it till I jumped off that bed. It shore is high."

"That's because there's a trundle bed under it. Now, let me have a look."

With gentle hands she carefully felt the ankle.

"You've got a bad sprain. We'll soak it in ice water, then wrap it well. I'm afraid you couldn't have hiked home today anyway. We're snowed in. I called friends in North Fork to get word to your grandfather that you are here."

"I'm obliged to you," the boy said.

He stuffed down two helpings of the scrambled eggs and bacon while the puffy ankle soaked in a pan of water. Then the woman carefully wrapped it in a wide elastic bandage.

"You take this cane," she said, "and explore the house to see what your grandfather helped to build. If your ankle begins to hurt, climb on a sofa and raise your ankle with some pillows. I'll read to you and we'll talk about your grandfather. When evening comes, if you like, I'll tell you the Christmas story."

It had been a full day, a fun day. By the time darkness fell, snow had covered the second rail of the fence outside the living room window. The woman lit a fire in the fireplace that was large enough for a boy to stand in. A Christmas tree with little white lights that twinkled against the old hewn logs reached to the beamed ceiling. The boy leaned back, a pillow tucked comfortably behind him, and another under the sprained ankle.

"I like your house," he said suddenly. "Feels like home."

"That's the nicest thing anyone could say about it," she said smiling. "It's fun dressing it up for Christmas—always has been. We have five children, and they're all married now with homes of their own. But we dress up Little Piney Cove for Jesus' birthday every Christmas, and if any of them can come home they're more than welcome."

"Got any grandkids?"

"Nineteen."

"Goleee!" the boy exclaimed. "Just like some mountain folks."

"Thank you, Zeb. I consider that a real compliment. You know," she continued, eyes smiling, "there's a gift for you under the tree."

"For me?" Gray eyes widened in surprise.

Among the piles of gifts awaiting the family's arrival, she picked up a long, skinny one wrapped in bright red with a shiny ribbon.

Slowly he opened it. Unused to gifts, he didn't want to spoil the ribbon or tear the paper. There across his lap lay a walking stick made from a vine-strangled sapling.

"It was here when we bought the place," explained the woman. "They said it belonged to your grandfather. When you showed up last night, I remembered it. I said to myself, 'This stick ought to belong to Zeb.'"

The boy's hands felt along the curved groove left by the vine, his eyes bright.

"I shore am pleased t' get it," the boy said, "mighty pleased . . ." and he couldn't say anymore.

"Now," the woman announced, "the Christmas story!"

In The Beginning

The woman put a log on the fire, which exploded into hundreds of tiny red stars. They twinkled against the sooty back of the fireplace and disappeared up the chimney.

"The first Christmas happened almost 2,000 years ago," she began. "That's when the angel appeared to shepherds outside Bethlehem. But the story doesn't begin there. It couldn't have because the angel called Jesus a 'savior,' or a rescuer. Someone must have been in trouble.

"To find out about it, we have to jump into a time machine and go back before Mary and Joseph were born. Back before there was any town of Bethlehem. In fact, so far back there was no earth. (Whoops—now our time machine has nothing to sit on!)"

She glanced at him, and the boy grinned back. Then she continued.

In the beginning, the earth was shapeless and empty; and darkness was over the face of the deep. Then God began to move.

"Light!" God commanded in a voice that cracked like thunder. There was a brilliant flash, and God separated the light from the darkness.

Next He set the sun, moon and stars in their orbits. Then He shaped our earth and began filling it with wonders. He scooped out deep oceans and heaped up high mountains. In the oceans He put huge fish, prickly sea urchins, octopuses and great sea turtles. On the mountains He set down goats, bears and bobcats. The valleys and plains He filled with all sorts of surprises: porcupines, tigers, parrots and deer, then rhinoceroses, giraffes and warthogs.

You couldn't count all the creatures He made. Some looked like they were made with love; others with a chuckle. Some even looked like a bad joke. And not one was exactly like any other. It was a real zoo.

Then came the most exciting moment of all. God made a man and a woman to rule over all He had made. He called the man Adam, and the woman He called Eve. He brought all His creatures to Adam so the man could give them names. Whatever Adam decided to call them, that became their name—whether an owl, a whale or a pig. Adam must have had a ball!

God was enjoying Adam and Eve; in fact, He loved them more than anything else He had created.

He chose the most beautiful spot on earth for them to live—the Garden of Eden. And He gave Adam and Eve everything they needed to be happy. They had crystal-clear rivers to drink from and swim in; nuts and berries to eat; vines to swing on; flowers to smell and birds to sing them songs. They didn't need clothes, and were not embarrassed.

They didn't need spears or slings, for they had no enemies. The lions purred instead of growling. Horses and hyenas came loping and leaping when Adam called because they knew he was their loving master.

Adam and Eve had a wonderful time as they pruned branches and turned the soil around the plants. Working was fun, and they never grew tired. In the afternoon when the last tool was put away, Adam and Eve would run with the antelope, swim with the otter and sing with the oriole.

The best part always came in the cool of the day. As the leaves began to dance in the gentle evening breezes, God would walk with Adam and Eve in the Garden.

Everything was beautiful; it looked like all would live happily ever after.

———————————

The woman's voice trailed off. She sat silent, thinking.

"Did they?" the boy asked.

"No. I'm afraid not," she said. "For soon, something was about to go terribly wrong in the Garden."

CHAPTER 4

THE TESTING TREE

The woman paused briefly and adjusted the cushion near the boy's ankle. Tickled that the cat was curled up on Zeb's chest, she tended the fire and began again.

In the very center of the Garden of Eden, God planted a beautiful tree. Prettier than any Christmas tree, its ornaments were a strange and lovely fruit. But this tree was off-limits to Adam and Eve. For this was the Testing Tree.

God put it there on purpose, to test and see whether Adam and Eve would obey Him.

Of course, He could have made humans more like other creatures, which do things without question. A caterpillar does not ask himself, "Let's see, shall I spin myself into a cocoon and turn into a butterfly? Or is it more fun to be a caterpillar?" He just does what he does and cannot do otherwise.

God had decided He wouldn't get much pleasure from humans who acted like caterpillars. He wanted people who would obey Him and be His children because they *chose* to.

And so the Testing Tree! It wasn't a hard test—not like putting a candy bar in front of you and saying you mustn't eat it. After all, there were lots of other trees in the Garden of Eden. Plenty of juicy apples and oranges to choose from, and figs, grapes, cherries, plums—better than the best candy bars.

God told Adam to help himself to all but that one tree in the middle of the Garden. "For if you eat of it," He said, "you will surely die." This is when all the trouble started.

One day, a serpent slipped through the bushes and whispered to Eve in a smooth, silky voice, "Did God really say, 'You must not eat from any tree in the Garden'?"

"Oh, no," Eve replied. "We can eat from most trees. But the fruit that grows on the tree in the middle of the Garden is not for us. God told us that if we eat it, we will die."

The serpent's forked tongue flicked out and about as he said slyly "S-s-urely you won't die. God knows when you eat it you will begin to understand secrets. You will become as wise as He is. Just take it," the serpent urged.

This serpent, as you might already know, was no ordinary snake. It was really a disguise—a costume—for Satan himself. Satan had once been an angel called "son of the morning." But he was a real troublemaker, and in his pride he had begun to want to be as great and wise as God Himself. So Satan fell from heaven, sending shock waves still felt today.

Now, seeing Adam and Eve whom God loved, Satan thought of a way to get even. A way to spoil God's plan.

To Eve, the snake's words sounded exciting. She ran to the center of the

Garden and looked up into the branches of the Testing Tree. There, ripe and tempting, hung the fruit. She remembered what Satan said about it making her as wise as God.

So she picked one. For a moment, she wondered if it would really kill her. She took a tiny bite of it, and waited. Nothing happened. She waited some more. Still nothing. Eve felt as strong as ever, and the fruit was so sweet! Quickly she gulped down the rest of it. Then picking a piece for Adam, she took it to him. Adam ate it.

And joy died; fear came.

That doesn't sound too awful, does it? No worse, anyway, than stealing cookies from the cookie jar. But this was the first time anyone on earth had ever disobeyed God. And from that day on, all was ruined.

When Adam and Eve failed the test at the Testing Tree, it may not have been the end of the world. It *was*, however, the end of the happiness His world had enjoyed. Every horrible thing you can think of—sickness, war, loneliness, thorns, nightmares—got its start the moment Eve disobeyed God. And since God loved His children, He already knew He would come to our rescue. From the beginning of time, we needed Christmas.

Meanwhile God had to deal with Adam and his wife.

Now, where had they disappeared to?

${\cal E}$DEN ${\cal L}$OST CHAPTER 5

The boy's eyes were solemn as he listened. The cat, no longer curled up, was sprawled out across the boy, sound asleep.

"Would you like a cup of hot chocolate?" the woman asked.

"No, thank you, ma'am. What happened next?"

That evening, in the cool of the day, Adam and Eve walked in the Garden. "Adam," God called, "where are you?"

Adam and Eve looked at each other in terror. Always before they had run to meet Him. But now they were shaking. For the first time, they did not want to be near God. They wanted to run away, to put their fingers in their ears and pretend they didn't hear Him.

So they dashed behind some trees and waited, hoping God would go away. It had been like this all day. Waiting . . . feeling afraid . . . waiting . . . feeling guilty . . . waiting some more. Sure, when they tasted the fruit that morning, nothing seemed to happen. Yet God's words kept echoing in their minds: "If you eat the fruit, you will die."

Perhaps, they thought, *God did not really mean it. After all, we are still alive, aren't we?*

But when God said they would die, He meant their friendship with Him would die. They would want to live without Him. And they would die inside.

So they did. Adam and Eve started to feel things they had never felt before—rotten things like fear and anger and shame. Their bodies slowly began to get older. They felt tired, even sick at times—a hint that, sooner or later, their earthly lives would be no more.

And God knew that after this death there awaited a death that would never end.

Adam slowly came out from behind the trees. Trembling, he said to God, "I heard Your voice in the Garden and was afraid."

"Have you eaten from the tree I told you not to eat?" God asked.

Adam replied, "The woman You gave me—she gave me some fruit from the tree and I ate it."

"Eve!" God said sternly. "What is it that you and Adam have done?"

"The snake did it!" Eve protested. "He talked me into it! It was his fault!"

But God is not impressed by excuses. All three had "sinned"—which means they had disobeyed Him. And all three had to be punished.

God turned first to the snake. "You will crawl on your belly and eat dust all the days of your life." Ever since then, as you well know, snakes have slithered along the ground.

Turning to Adam and Eve, God said, "Now you will find life hard; you must leave the Garden." Then He made coats of skins to clothe them, for they were ashamed.

Adam and Eve looked with horror at the skins. They recognized the fur; it had belonged to their animal friends.

Darkness fell. Over the Garden swept a great storm—low, black clouds boiling. The leaves of the Testing Tree began shaking, and all the other trees bent low in the howling wind. It struck Adam and Eve with such force, they ran to keep from falling.

So God drove them out of the Garden. At the entrance, He placed a tall angel with a flashing sword to block the way back.

Outside Eden, life was cold and hard. Instead of simply reaching up into the trees for dinner, Adam and Eve had to plant seeds and pull weeds to raise their own food. Working was exhausting. Thorns and bugs thrived. Rottenness, decay, germs—all these ugly things came as a result of Adam and Eve's sin. The earth and all who lived on it were under a curse.

The Garden of Eden had been Adam and Eve's home. But what really made them feel at home was the loving presence of their Heavenly Father. God Himself had been their true "home." Now all was lost. Adam and Eve were the world's first homeless people.

The Man Who Listened

That ain't the end," the boy said hopefully as he smoothed the purring cat. "No," the woman smiled. "It's just the beginning. You see, God was determined to make a way for man to come back Home. It happened like this....

God still loved these people He had made. For He does not change. No matter how badly Adam and Eve had sinned, they were still His. So, though He drove them from the Garden, He continued to watch over them.

Many years passed, and God kept watching over Adam and Eve. They had two sons, Cain and Abel. When these boys grew up, Cain killed Abel, his only brother. For the first time ever, Adam and Eve saw someone dead—and their own son at that! They wept till there were no tears left, and awoke the next day to weep again. They realized once more what a terrible thing it is to disobey God.

Adam and Eve had more children, and those children had children until there were whole cities of people—and most of them acted as badly as Cain. God kept looking for someone who would listen to Him and obey. Someone to whom He could be a friend. But they didn't listen. Just as the first two people forgot about God, so did those who came after them.

Instead of living in peace, they fought with each other. The soldier who killed the most people was the greatest hero. And when they weren't fighting, the children of Adam liked noisy pleasures. At their parties, they stuffed themselves, shouted and drank far into the night.

In all the noisy confusion people did not hear the voice of God speaking to their hearts. No one heard Him saying, over and over, that this was not the way to live, that this was not what He had created them for.

God saw how wicked the people had become; their thoughts were continually evil. It made Him very angry. Grieving, He decided to wash mankind from the face of the earth so He could start all over again.

In all that wickedness, one man stood out. For he was just and upright, a man who walked with God. His name was Noah. God decided to save Noah and his family from the flood that was coming. He told Noah to build an ark—a huge boat with many rooms inside. And God told him exactly how to build it.

It would be big enough to hold Noah's whole family plus some of every kind of animal and bird in the world.

When Noah's neighbors saw him building a huge boat on dry land, many miles from the ocean, they laughed until their sides hurt and tears rolled down their cheeks. But Noah didn't care what people thought; he wanted only to obey God.

After the last board was pegged in place, Noah and his three sons led the animals into the ark. His wife and his sons' wives carried in the food: seed for the birds, grain for the cattle and horses, dried fruit for themselves—enough

to last for a long, long time. As Noah and his family and the animals waited inside the ark, Noah's neighbors laughed louder than ever.

While they were laughing, the rain began to fall. Through the downpour, those in the ark heard a strange sound. The laughter had turned to wailing. Then the air was pierced by screams. Fists pounded on the outside of the ark. Noah and his family could do nothing, for God had shut them in. Soon the pounding stopped, cries grew fewer and then there was only the steady pouring of rain.

Day and night the raging storm continued. In the flickering light of their oil lamps inside the ark, Noah's family sat and listened to the rain pounding on the roof. After many days they felt the ark gently rocking, and they knew it was floating on the water.

It rained for forty days and forty nights. When at last it stopped, Noah opened the window to look out. There was nothing but water, stretching as far as his eyes could see. Not even the mountain peaks showed.

Several weeks passed while they floated on. The animals wished they could get out and run. The deer paced back and forth in their stalls. The ark began to smell as bad as a dirty barn on a hot August day. Noah and his family wondered if they would ever see dry land again!

Then one day Noah opened the window and lifted out a dove. The dove eagerly took to the skies. It flapped its wings and soared above the water until it was out of sight. Several hours later the dove returned, holding an olive leaf in its beak. That made all the animals in the ark very happy, because they knew the water must finally be going down.

A whole year went by before the earth was dry enough to walk on. Then

out of the ark they all tumbled, Noah and his family and all the animals. The cows kicked up their hooves and bounded across the hills as though spring had come after a long winter. Noah's family was so glad to get out of the crowded ark, they wanted to run and jump and turn cartwheels. But before he did anything else, Noah built an altar and offered a solemn prayer of thanks to God.

God promised Noah and his family that He would never again destroy the earth with a flood. And He placed a rainbow in the sky as a sign that He would never forget His promise.

At first, the people didn't forget either. Noah's sons remembered God and the great flood He had sent. They told their own sons and daughters about it. And the sons and daughters told their children—but it was starting to seem like a story from long, long ago. People could no longer recall exactly why Noah and his family were rescued from the flood. They forgot how important it was to listen to God.

God intended for everyone to live together in peace. But people began once again to stray from His plan. If a man was strong, he would take all the wheat from his neighbor's fields and all the fruit from his trees and lock them up in his own storehouses. The strongest and richest declared themselves rulers, making whole cities their slaves.

They invented many fake gods: a god to help them win wars, a god to make it rain, a god to chase wolves away. They even tried to imagine what these gods looked like; they carved them out of wood, stone, even metal.

Watching the people, God saw they were getting more confused all the time. "There is only *one* God!" He kept trying to tell them.

It was no use. They didn't hear Him. Most people had ignored God for so long, they didn't even recognize His voice.

God thought of another plan to rescue His people—a plan that would one day lead to that first Christmas in Bethlehem. To make the plan work, God needed someone who was still faithful to Him.

And He knew just where to find him.

THE CHOSEN PEOPLE

Abraham lived in a rich and beautiful city called Haran. He was one of the few people who still listened to God. One day he heard God's voice say:

Get out of your country,...to a land that I will show you. I will make you a great nation;...in you all the families of the earth shall be blessed. *(Genesis 12:1-3)*

Abraham was seventy-five years old. Leaving home was hard, but he obeyed God. Taking his whole family, he traveled by camelback to the new land.

For many years Abraham and his family lived in that country, which was called Canaan. Then, during the life of his grandson Jacob (also called Israel), there came a great famine. To find food, Israel and his children left their homes and moved south to Egypt.

Here they settled. At first the Egyptians welcomed them, but after many years they turned against them and made them slaves. For hundreds of years the Israelites sweated and strained for the Egyptians. It seemed as if God had forgotten His promise to make them a great nation.

Egypt was a rich nation; its king, the Pharaoh, had more slaves and more gold than any other ruler. The Egyptians believed in many false gods and built huge temples for them. Many of the Israelite slaves began worshiping the idols of Egypt.

All day the Israelites would slave in the mud pits, making bricks for the Egyptians. Then at night, while their masters were chanting and singing in the great temples, they went back to their tiny shacks. Those who still believed in the one true God prayed to Him in whispers.

God hears whispers just as well as shouts. He lives in slums as well as in palaces. And He heard the Israelites' desperate prayers for help. Even though these descendants of Noah had disappointed God, He still loved them. So, once again, He prepared a leader to rescue His people. God found a faithful man named Moses and told him, "I am sending you to Pharaoh to bring My people out of Egypt."

Moses knew Pharaoh would be furious when he heard the plan. After all, why should a king agree to let his valuable slaves go free? But Moses obeyed God. He went bravely to Pharaoh and said, "Thus says the Lord God of Israel: 'Let my people go!'"

As Moses expected, Pharaoh turned red with anger. "Who is this *Lord*," he roared, "that I should obey *His* voice to let Israel go?" In his fury, Pharaoh made the children of Israel work harder than ever. To make Pharaoh change his mind, God sent many plagues on Egypt. One was a plague of frogs. Green, slimy frogs—thousands and thousands of them—covered the ground. They were everywhere the Egyptians stepped. Frogs hopped into their beds and jumped into the dough when the cooks tried to make bread.

The Egyptians prayed desperately to all their gods to take the frogs away. The sound of croaking only grew louder.

At last Pharaoh begged Moses to pray to *his* God. "If your God takes the frogs away," he promised, "I will let your people go."

He was lying. When God took the frogs away, Pharaoh only laughed—and he didn't let the people go.

So God sent more plagues to the Egyptians: gnats, flies, boils, hail, locusts. Everywhere, people were itching and swatting and scratching and ducking hailstones. And they began to starve because the locusts had eaten all the food.

Now God told His own people how to survive the most dreadful plague of all.

Each household was to get a perfect little lamb. When they had killed it, they were to put blood on each side of the door and on the top. God called this His Passover. For wherever He saw the blood, His Destroyer passed over that house.

On that dark night, all the firstborn sons of the Egyptians died. Pharaoh was awakened by the terrible sound of weeping. His wife was holding their dead son. Through her tears, she glared at him accusingly.

All over the land, as mothers discovered their dead sons, cries arose until all that could be heard was unbroken wailing. Now Pharaoh was truly terrified. He sent for Moses, then begged him to take his people and leave at once.

So the children of Israel—well over a million of them—grabbed their belongings and hurried out of Egypt as fast as their legs could go. But once more Pharaoh changed his mind. While the Israelites were resting at the edge of the Red Sea, Pharaoh and his army came chasing after them.

The sea lay in front of the Israelites, and the dust cloud of Pharaoh's powerful army was quickly closing in from behind. They were trapped! Suddenly there came a mighty east wind. All that night God blew back the water of the sea until a dry path appeared right through the middle of it, with the water a wall on either side.

The children of Israel hurried through the opening in the

water. When the Egyptians tried to cross after them, the water rushed back in with a thunderous crash. Armor and chariots crashed and shattered. Horses reared, rolling their eyes and snorting in terror as they threw their riders. Then all fell silent except for the lapping of the waves along the shore. Pharaoh's mighty army was never seen or heard from again.

At last the children of Israel were safe, and they were free to worship the one true God. On a mountaintop on the other side of the sea, God gave Moses the Ten Commandments and other laws to help His chosen people know how to live.

In time God led them to the land He had given Abraham many years before. It was to this land, and among these people, that God planned to send a Savior to rescue the human race once and for all. God had chosen the people and the place, but He was waiting for the right time.

———————————

The grandfather clock struck 10. The woman looked up.

The fire had dwindled to a heap of glowing coals.

The boy was watching her with wide eyes, but there were shadows under them.

"Well, I never!" she exclaimed. "Time crept up on us while we were in Egypt, I guess."

"It's interestin'," the boy protested.

"It can wait until morning," the woman said. "Come, have a cup of hot milk and some pie and then hit the hay."

She set about getting the kitchen ready for the next morning. Meanwhile the boy, with his sprained ankle soaking in the pan again, ate the pie and washed it down with warm milk.

"Sleep well, Zeb," she said as he got up to go to the guest room.

"'Night, ma'am, and thank you for today."

Trouble Chapter 8
After Trouble

Early the next morning the boy woke to the still whitened world—snowflakes tumbling down thickly.

Easing himself down the steps beside the high bed, he limped across to the kitchen where the familiar smells of breakfast welcomed him.

"Good morning, Zeb." The woman smiled. "Sleep well? Good. We're snowed in for another day. The weatherman says it is the worst storm in ten years."

"I don't mind," the boy grinned. "It's nice 'n warm in here."

"I love a snowstorm."

"Me too," the boy agreed. "And when you're not too busy, maybe we can finish the Christmas story."

"Good! I've built the living room fire. When you're ready you light it. Not much to do on a day like this, so we'll just have fun."

"Now where were we?" the woman asked as she joined him.

"The people had gotten out of Egypt to a land God had given them. God was awaitin' for somethin'."

"That's right," the woman replied.

God had led His children to the land called Canaan. It was the same land God had given to Abraham hundreds of years before. But now, wicked people lived there.

They worshiped a false god, Baal, which led them to do foul, evil things. Once again, some of God's people left Him and began worshiping Baal.

To punish them, God let enemies conquer and carry away His children. Each time they would be sorry for their disobedience and call on God to rescue them. And God would. But since their sorrow never lasted, they were punished over and over again.

To help rescue the people when they strayed, God raised up leaders called judges. They were more like army generals than court judges.

One, famous for his strength, was Samson. His greatest victory came after God's enemies had captured him and put out his eyes. One day, thousands gathered in a temple to worship their god, Dagon. Thousands more were on the roof. Drunk with wine, they sent for Samson to make fun of him. When they finished, Samson braced himself between two central pillars. With a cry to God for strength, he pushed with all his might. Down came the roof killing thousands of people, including blind Samson.

Israel's last judge

was Samuel. When Samuel grew old, all the elders of Israel came to him. "You're old now," they said. "Make us a king like all the other nations." Samuel answered, "But you already have a king; God Himself is your King!"

"We want a king we can see," they demanded. "A king like other countries have."

Samuel did not like this, and he prayed to God.

"Listen to the people," God said. "They haven't rejected you; they have rejected Me." So Israel received a king named Saul. Saul was tall and handsome and *looked* like a king. But he soon turned away from God, so God left him.

For Israel's next king, God chose a shepherd boy named David. David was the young man who killed the wicked giant Goliath with only a pebble and sling, and cut off Goliath's head with his own sword. David also wrote many songs to God that the Bible calls "psalms." God loved David in a very special way. The Bible calls him "the man after God's own heart."

When David died, his son Solomon became king. God loved Solomon too, and gave him great wisdom. But as Solomon grew older, he began to forget God. He even offered burnt sacrifices to false gods. And many of the Israelites followed his bad example.

Then God sent men called prophets to try to win back the hearts of His people. "If you do not turn from your evil ways," the prophets said, "God will let other nations conquer you." Many nations were eager to do just that, because the Israelites had some of the best land.

Despite the prophets' warnings, God's children didn't obey. So He finally allowed them to be conquered. Their capital city, Jerusalem, was destroyed, and most of the people were taken away to be slaves in a place called Babylon. Everything looked hopeless for the Israelites. In God's eyes, however, there *was* still hope. For even in Babylon, a few people remembered God and prayed to Him.

One of these was a young nobleman named Daniel. He kept praying to God even when it was against the law. So they threw him into a den of hungry lions. Do you remember the surprise ending of that story? God shut the lions' mouths, and they missed their dinner!

Like Daniel, others remained faithful. And God sent them a wonderful promise:

> The people who walked in darkness have seen a great light;
> those who dwelt in the land of the shadow of death, upon
> them a light has shined.... For unto us a Child is born, unto us
> a Son is given; and the government will be upon His shoulder.
> And His name will be called Wonderful, Counselor, Mighty
> God, Everlasting Father, Prince of Peace. *(Isaiah 9:2,6)*

The Son of God was finally coming to rescue them—coming to be their Savior! But *when* would He come? How much longer would God's children have to wait for that first Christmas morning?

Even the angels didn't know.

The Time Grows Short

CHAPTER 9

Since Jesus would be born in Israel, at first only the Israelites would know about Him. But God would want them to tell others, who in turn would tell even more people, until the whole world had heard about Jesus. It would be easier if many people spoke the same language.

They had to be able to travel to distant places, too, so the furthest city and the countries beyond the sea could hear. For that, they needed good roads and strong ships.

Still it was not time. Hundreds of years went by. That might seem to us like a long time to wait, but what takes a year on earth is to God only the blinking of an eye.

Finally a city called Rome was built. The armies of Rome conquered all the countries around, including Israel.

To make sure all the conquered people obeyed them, the Romans built roads for their armies. These stone paths were bigger and better than any roads the people had ever seen. The Romans also built hundreds of fast, sturdy ships and chased pirates off the seas.

50

One of the countries Rome conquered was Greece. The language of Greece sounded so beautiful that many people throughout the Roman Empire began to speak it. And God, listening, knew that Greek would be a perfect language for spreading the news of His rescue.

God had already said His Son would be born in Israel. And through the prophet Micah, God revealed the exact place where this Savior would be born:

> But you Bethlehem, . . . though you are little, . . . out of you shall
> come forth to Me the One to be ruler in Israel. *(Micah 5:2)*

Even though the children of Israel were finally back in their homelands, they were being ruled by the wicked emperors of Rome. Now, God was saying, they would have their very own King once again. This was wonderful news. And He would be the best ruler they could possibly have, for He would be the One chosen by God.

God was ready to show into whose family this new ruler would be born. Though God was His Father, He would need an earthly mother.

Who would be just right as a mother for God's Son? God chose a pure, simple girl named Mary—a girl who loved God with all her heart, mind, body and soul.

Mary looked up one day, startled. There before her stood a tall angel. Seeing her expression, the angel said kindly, "Peace to you who are lovingly chosen. The Lord is with you. Blessed are you among women."

> You will conceive in your womb and bring forth a Son, and
> shall call His name JESUS. He will be great, and will be
> called the Son of the Highest. . . . He will reign over the
> house of Jacob forever, and of His kingdom there will be no
> end. *(Luke 1:31-33)*

Mary was amazed; she could hardly speak. But she had always loved God. She tried not only to obey Him but also to please Him in everything. So she bowed low, saying to the angel, "I am the Lord's servant. . . . May it be to me as you have said."

Mary was engaged to a kind, strong man named Joseph. He could trace his relatives back to the great King David. Joseph was only a poor carpenter in Nazareth. But he married Mary and cared for her tenderly as the time drew near for her baby to be born.

Nazareth, where Joseph and Mary lived, was almost a hundred miles from *Bethlehem*—a long, long distance in those days! But the prophet Micah had predicted that the Savior would be born in Bethlehem. How could this come true?

The emperor in Rome at that time was Caesar Augustus—meaning "Caesar the Splendid." One day Caesar decided to count all the people in his huge empire. That way he would know how much tax money he could collect from them. To keep track of all the different groups of people, Caesar decided people should go back to the town where they were born and pay taxes *there*.

Well, when Caesar Augustus decided something, it became law. He did not know it was God who gave him the idea. All over the Roman world, people had to return to their hometowns to pay their taxes. It was hard for some to do this, but when Caesar said "Go!" people went.

And that's how Joseph and Mary ended up in Bethlehem.

———————————————

"God shore went through a heap of trouble," Zeb said. "More than I'd a done."

"More than any of us would have done," agreed the woman.

THE FIRST CHRISTMAS

What if we had lived in Bethlehem at the time Jesus was born? Our story might have been like that of a boy named Aaron and his little sister Anna.

They loved all the excitement in this normally sleepy town. There was something going on everywhere they looked. And the people! They had never seen so many people!

Out on the narrow, crowded street, dusty men tugged and shouted at heavily-laden donkeys. Aaron grinned to himself as he watched the sweat make stripes on their faces. Women with tiny children were everywhere. Older children were lugging bundles of food. Everyone looked weary, since the only reason they had come here was to pay unfair taxes.

Aaron and Anna's favorite place was the city gate. Late one afternoon they climbed up onto the sun-warmed wall to watch strangers come into town.

Alone and in groups the people arrived, some walking rapidly on this last bit of their journey. An old man at the gate said a few of the travelers were from as far away as Nazareth. Aaron could hardly believe it; they must have spent four or five nights sleeping beside the road.

The afternoon sun felt good on Aaron's and Anna's backs, for the air was a little chilly. Anna became sleepy and closed her eyes. Minutes later, Aaron nudged her and she awoke. Two people were coming up the dusty road in the valley, a man walking and a woman riding a donkey. They traveled so slowly. The woman had her hand on the man's shoulder, and she seemed very tired. The man kept looking at her anxiously.

As the couple drew closer, Aaron and Anna could see that their donkey was covered with dust. They had come a long way. But why did they stop so often, when their trip was almost over? They paused again, right in front of the gate. The woman looked up at the children and smiled. Their hearts filled with wonder!

The young woman's face—her eyes great pools of darkness—was pale with exhaustion. But it held a tender smile that made the children forget taxes and Roman soldiers and even Caesar Augustus himself. In hot, noisy, crowded Bethlehem, her smile seemed to say that all the joy in heaven had come down to earth.

That night, wrapped up in his cloak, Aaron couldn't sleep. All he could think of was that smile—that incredible smile. It was unusual, those days, to see a happy face, much less a beautiful smile. He wondered if the man and woman had found a place to sleep.

Aaron stirred restlessly; he somehow knew this was a special night. Something wonderful, he sensed, was about to happen. Something so wonderful he was almost afraid to breathe.

Bethlehem was very still. On other evenings, donkeys brayed in their stables and wolves howled from the hilltops. But even the donkeys and wolves were quiet. The wind itself had stopped blowing. It was as if the whole world was listening—waiting.

Late, very late, there was a commotion outside. Men were shouting and running, their sandals scuffing on the dirt. Aaron poked Anna, his finger on his lips. Quietly, the children jumped to their feet and ran to the door.

They stared at the men talking so loudly in the middle of the night. Not only their shaggy hair and ragged robes but also their smell marked them as shepherds. Probably the outcast shepherds who kept watch over the sheep outside Bethlehem—the sheep chosen for the temple sacrifices.

But what were they saying? They had seen an *angel?*

Aaron looked at them again to make sure they were really shepherds and not crazy people. "We saw an angel!" they repeated. "And the angel told us about a baby being born in Bethlehem—a baby called 'Savior' and 'Lord.'" They had just seen the baby with their *own eyes!* He was in a cave that the innkeeper used for a stable.

Aaron didn't wait to hear more. Grabbing Anna's hand, he took off down the street as fast as he could run. Anna's short legs could hardly keep up with his longer ones. They ran past houses where drowsy people stumbled to the doors to see what all the racket was about. Panting, they finally reached the cave and peered in.

There she was—the woman with the radiant smile! She was lying on soft hay piled beside one of the stalls. Her eyes were closed, but her peaceful smile filled the cave with wonder. The man knelt by her side and covered her gently

with his cloak. And next to them, in the feeding trough for the cows, lay the baby.

He seemed so tiny, wrapped tight in a long linen band and sleeping soundly like any other baby. He slept as though the world had not waited thousands of years for that moment. As though Aaron's and Anna's lives and those of everyone on earth were not wrapped up in His birth. As though all the sin and sorrow of the world was not His concern.

Aaron wondered if he dared speak to the young mother, but he didn't want to disturb her. He wanted to ask her if he could touch the baby. Not to wake Him, but just to touch Him.

Then Aaron looked at his own grubby hands. He couldn't remember when he had last washed them. So he tucked them behind his back and just looked.

Aaron glanced at Anna. Little Anna was on her knees, her hands clasped together, a look of surprise and joy on her face. Tears were trickling down her grimy little cheeks.

Aaron knelt beside her.

It Is Finished

Zeb sat still for a while, staring at the Christmas tree. Then he spoke quietly. "Ma'am, what I don't get is how a *baby* could save a world. Can you explain that?"

"Good question!" the woman replied. "You've probably heard some wonderful stories about Jesus' life—the parables He told and the miracles He performed. But it's what happened at the *end* of His life that matters most. Let's pick up the story of Aaron and Anna, after they had grown up. It's Passover time in Jerusalem."

"The same Passover they did in Egypt?" Zeb asked.

"Yes," the woman replied. "They were celebrating how God had delivered them from Egypt. But this Passover was the most important of all, as you will soon see."

Having heard about Jesus all their lives, Aaron and Anna could not believe the news of His arrest. They, like many others, believed Jesus would rescue them from the Romans.

Now Jesus was sentenced to die.

On that day crowds began gathering on the hill called "the Place of the Skull." Aaron studied the people. The hardened soldiers, used to suffering and death, sat and gambled. The arrogant centurion in charge stood near them—efficient, unfeeling. The mocking scribes and Pharisees were there too. But most of the people were just curious onlookers who had come to Jerusalem to celebrate the Passover.

Anna spotted a small group off to one side near the center cross. Something about one of the women drew her attention. The woman looked up, and the sun shone straight on her face. Anna tugged Aaron's sleeve. The woman was older now, but there was no mistaking even at this distance: She was the mother they had seen in the cave.

How long they stood there Aaron never knew. He felt in some way that he himself was dying. Everything was growing dark—darker—till it was black as midnight. The earth began to shake. Aaron gripped Anna's arm. After a while, the shaking stopped but the darkness lingered for three long hours. The scoffers stopped scoffing. The crowds grew quiet.

And in that awful stillness, a single loud cry arose.

"My God! My God! Why have You forsaken Me?"

No answer. Only silence. Then the same voice, exclaiming, "It is finished!"

The figure on the cross slumped.

Aaron drew in his breath as Anna sobbed.

But somehow they couldn't bear to leave. In the strangely dim light, a well-dressed man came with some soldiers to take Jesus' body down from the cross. They put Him in a tomb in a nearby garden and rolled a huge stone across the entrance.

Wordlessly, Aaron and Anna made their way home.

The boy sat gazing thoughtfully into the fireplace.

"That just naturally ain't right. Sounds like He didn't rescue no one. Just up and died."

"I know it sounds that way," the woman said. "And the following day must have been one of the saddest in history. All Jesus' followers hid for fear of the Jewish leaders. His friends had believed Jesus was the one who would free them from the Romans. Now they were frightened and disappointed. But the *next* morning something happened."

Before dawn, a great earthquake shook the land. The angel of the Lord descended like lightning, his clothes white as snow. Ignoring the Roman guards, he tossed back the huge stone and calmly sat on it. The soldiers shook with terror and fell like dead men.

Two of the women who had followed Jesus came at dawn and found the tomb empty. They clutched each other in fear. "Don't be afraid," the angel said. "Jesus has risen. Now go and tell all His disciples."

Jesus showed Himself to all His disciples and friends like Aaron and Anna over the next few weeks—in the garden, on the road to Emmaus, in the upper room where they'd been hiding and beside the Sea of Galilee.

Sitting down with them all, He told them not to blame the Jewish leaders, the Romans or anyone else for His crucifixion. He explained how ever since the Garden of Eden, God had tried to tell people He was going to send them a Savior.

And Jesus was that Savior.

God did not send Him to deliver them from unjust rulers, from illness or unpleasant situations. He was born to die, to die for the sins of mankind. Those who were sorry for their sins, even the worst of people, could be forgiven. And they once more would know the joy of companionship with God lost so long ago in Eden.

Through His death and resurrection, the baby born that night in Bethlehem had become Lord of all.

This is the real meaning of Christmas, the joy and glory of it!

———————————

It was still dark when Zeb awoke the next morning. He wasn't even sure he had been asleep because his head was so full of all he had heard that wintry night. He lay thinking for a long time.

Climbing carefully down the steps from the high bed, he hopped over to the window and pulled back the curtain. One bright star was twinkling in the sky.

It was dawn.

Acknowledgments by Ruth Bell Graham
My warmest thanks to all who helped on this project.
To Ray Seldomridge, a splendid and candid editor.
To Evelyn Freeland and Kathryn Morgan for patiently typing the manuscript through many changes.
To Steve Griffith for introducing me to Richard Jesse Watson.
To Dwight Baker for his expertise and encouragement.
And of course, to Richard Jesse Watson, an artist who has been a joy to work with and who has become a warm, personal friend.
May this story become a part of your family as it has been a part of ours.

Acknowledgments by Richard Jesse Watson
I am deeply grateful to those who helped make this a book of many miracles: To Susi, my wife and most cherished friend on earth,
and to Jesse, Faith, and Ben, my loving children and awesome friends. I so appreciate you, Ruth Bell Graham, for your delightful
friendship, encouragement, and solid prayers. Huge thanks to Steve Griffith for vision, insight, and friendship; to Ray Seldomridge,
pal, word juggler fantastique; to Don Aylard, a true Narnian and fine designer. Special thanks to Connie Gustafson Smiley for
exquisite calligraphy. My sincere gratitude to Dwight Baker and everyone at Baker Book House for patience and support, and to all
those at B. G. E. A. who in quiet ways played a vital part. The following folk were fabulous facilitators: my mom, Elsie M. Watson,
Maury Scobee, Rick Halverson, Roy Gustafson, Elias of Bethlehem, Karen Bretz, Joy Chu, the wild-feathered Hunts, the Al Morris
"fam", Mike White (for egging me on), Paul Boyer photography, Dan Lagasse, the Pratts and Alphy, Bergantz florist, Huntington
Gardens, and Marty Gay. For modeling, many thanks to Mark J. Lilly, T. G. Wazo, Jesse Buffalo, Luke Hunt, Chester, David Haskell,
Ethan Alley, Jason Ensminger, Rose Gonzales, Thomas Atkens, Frank Martinez, Jennifer Lynn Minish, Ashley Lloyd, Preacher Spider
H. Najera, Mikey A. M. Hernandez, James E. Everett, and Elme Lopez. I am humbled and grateful for the prayers of many—to those I
have not met and to Paddy Harrigian and friends, also the Harmsworths, Kristiana Gregory, Eddie Van Cleve, Arielle and Erik Baker
and family, Rick and Linda Larson, Jim and Marian Gilliland, Jim and Connie Rosenquist, and the Port Townsend Calvary Chapel.
Last and first, I give thanks to the Author of Life, and Illustrator of Glory, my Jesus.

Illustrations in this book were done in egg tempera on Strathmore illustration board.
The display type was hand-lettered by Connie Gustafson Smiley.
The text type was set in 12 point Caxton Book.
Printed by KHL Printing Co Pte Ltd
Separations by Modern Imaging
Production supervision by Dwight Baker and Stephen Price
Designed by Don Aylard

Standard edition ISBN 0-8010-3848-0
Deluxe edition ISBN 0-8010-1130-2

Third printing, August 1996

Printed and bound in Singapore
Worldwide coedition by Angus Hudson Ltd, London

Scripture quotations are from *The New King James* version,
copyright 1979 by Thomas Nelson Inc., Publishers.

Library of Congress Cataloging-in-Publication Data

Graham, Ruth Bell.
One wintry night: the Christmas story / Ruth Bell Graham;
illustrated by Richard Jesse Watson.
p.   cm.
Summary: Retells the Christmas story in a contemporary setting,
beginning with creation and closing with Christ's resurrection.
ISBN 0-8010-3848-0
1. Jesus Christ—Nativity—Juvenile literature. 2. Christmas—
Juvenile literature. [1. Jesus Christ. 2. Christmas.]
I. Watson, Richard Jesse, ill. II. Title.
BT315.2.G73 1994
232.92'1—dc20   91-48107